Literacy for Childcare Students

A Basic Skills Guide

Excellence in Childcare

Series Editor: Maureen Smith

This book is part of the Excellence in Childcare Series. The series is designed to support students and NVQ candidates, practitioners, managers and trainers to develop their skills and offer a high quality service to children and families.

Books in the series are written by experts with many years' experience of and commitment to the childcare sector. As the sector grows and develops, there is a demand not only for more childcare provision, but for better quality provision. The sector now requires very well qualified, excellent practitioners who can support children's development throughout the preschool years. The series aims to help new and established practitioners become confident, imaginative, excellent professionals.

Literacy for Childcare Students

A Basic Skills Guide

June Green

 David Fulton Publishers

David Fulton Publishers Ltd
The Chiswick Centre, 414 Chiswick High Road, London W4 5TF

www.fultonpublishers.co.uk

David Fulton Publishers is a division of Granada Learning Limited, part of the Granada Media group.

First published in Great Britain by David Fulton Publishers 2003
10 9 8 7 6 5 4 3 2 1

British Library Cataloguing in Publication Data
A catalogue record for this book is available from the British Library.

ISBN 1–84312–022–4

Typeset by FiSH Books, London
Printed and bound in Great Britain by Ashford Colour Press Limited, Gosport, Hants

Contents

Dedicated to my son, Radley
for all the support and encouragement, despite
the late and missed meals.
I couldn't have done it without you.

Welcome to the book

It's good to see you reading this.

As you are reading this there is a good chance that you are doing a childcare course and basic skills literacy. You probably have mixed feelings about the basic skills; most people do. I hope that what you read here will put your mind at rest.

Everyone needs basic skills to be able to get on in everyday life. We need to be able to read and write so that we can send text messages, read labels and directions, fill in forms. We need speaking and listening skills to talk on the phone. We may be able to do enough to get by in everyday life but what about if we want to do a course, get a job?

You have chosen to do a childcare course. As a childcare student/worker these skills are very important. Think about it. You will be working with children who are learning to read and write and to develop their speaking and listening skills. As a student you will be asked to support the children and the staff in developing these skills. How much easier it will be if you have developed your own skills first. How much more effective you will be in your work with the children. Think of the fun you can have reading a story to young children if you can make funny faces, put on different voices, read with tone – instead of having to work out what the words are. You won't have to think up excuses not to do it either, as one of my childcare students did for many months!

To work with children you need a childcare qualification. The higher level qualification you can get, the more choice you have with the jobs you can do. Doing the course means you will have assignments to do, notes to read, finding information from books and other resources, deadlines to meet! All this is easier to manage if you have good reading and writing skills. You will be asked to take part in and give presentations, take part in discussions and group work, give feedback. This is where the speaking and listening part of basic skill literacy comes in. Not only will it help you through your course but it will give you confidence in your day-to-day communication with children, parents, teachers and your own tutors.

So how can this basic skills literacy course help you? This course has been written by me, a childcare tutor, with you in mind. It is relevant to you, your life and to the course you are doing. Most of the activities are based around childcare, whether it is single words you will come across, looking for information or putting some work together. There are also tasks related to everyday life such as reading instructions, writing messages and directions to get somewhere.

This student book contains activities, reminders, spaces for dictionary work, spelling quizzes and so on that are all related to your basic skills class-work. You can use it to do extra activities in lessons or to work on in your own time.

'Why do I need this if I'm doing a course?' I hear you say. Well, I see one of the main aims of basic skills training as your being able to work independently. This workbook gives you the chance to do some independent work at a pace suited to you. If you find yourself speeding along in class you have some extra activities to do; if it takes you a little longer tackle these tasks in your own time and way. You can also see how you are progressing through the different levels. Why not set yourself a reward for each time you achieve something? It's a good excuse for a treat and a great motivator. I know – I've tried it. Everyone is different and I think that is one of the most important things to remember. This book can be used to suit you.

There are two pieces of advice I would like to give you and these come from students to whom I have taught basic skills:

1   Keep an open mind; this is not school work. Try and get rid of any unhappy or bad memories you have of doing English at school. This is a light-hearted, fun way of developing skills you already have to some extent and developing some new ones.
2   Do not compare yourself and your progress to anyone else. Everyone is different, everyone moves at a different pace. Watch and compare your own progress, not that of others. Your own progress and development is far more important than how everyone else is doing.

Literacy is not something to be scared of. Tackled in the right way it is fun and interesting. The activities you will be doing have been tried and tested on my own students and, believe me, they tell me when something is no good! As someone who struggled with reading and writing when I was at school I know how it feels when you think everyone can do better than you can, but you know, YOU CAN DO IT.

A last piece of advice from me – stick at it and HAVE FUN WHILE DOING SO!

Glossary

During your basic skills course, you will come across some unfamiliar words. Here is a list of some of those words and what they mean. Refer to it as you progress on through the levels – it will be useful.

It's called a *Glossary*, something you will come across in later levels!

Alphabet

- in <u>*UPPER CASE*</u> letters – A B C D E F G H I J K L M N O P Q R S T U V W X Y Z
- in <u>*lower case*</u> letters – a b c d e f g h i j k l m n o p q r s t u v w x y z

Consonants

- in <u>*UPPER CASE*</u> letters – B C D F G H J K L M N P Q R S T V W X Y Z
- in <u>*lower case*</u> letters – b c d f g h j k l m n p q r s t v w x y z

Vowels

- in <u>*UPPER CASE*</u> letters – A E I O U and sometimes Y
- written in <u>*lower case*</u> letters – a e i o u and sometimes y

Short vowel sounds

When the vowel makes its sound in a word, for example:

h<u>a</u>t   t<u>e</u>n   b<u>i</u>t   g<u>o</u>t   r<u>u</u>n

Long vowel sound

When the vowel makes the sound of its name in a word, for example:

n<u>a</u>me   th<u>e</u>se   n<u>i</u>ne   <u>o</u>nly   t<u>u</u>ne

Vowel phonemes

The smallest feature that makes a meaningful sound in a word, using at least one vowel, for example:

- t<u>o</u>, sh<u>oe</u> – both make the phoneme <u>oo</u>
- <u>air</u> : h<u>air</u>   <u>are</u> : r<u>are</u>   <u>ear</u> : w<u>ear</u> – all make the phoneme <u>air</u>

Root words

A word you can change by adding a prefix or suffix, for example:

The word *play* can be changed like this: adding 'ed' to the end = *play*ed or putting 'dis' before it = dis*play*

Prefix

A syllable added to the beginning of a root word to make another word, for example:

- *dis* added to *play* = *display*
- *un* added to *even* = *uneven*

Suffix

A syllable added to the end of a root word to make another word, for example:

- *ed* added to the end of *play* = *play**ed***
- *ly* added to the end of **friend** = **friend*ly***

Syllables

The part(s) of a word that can be spoken in one beat, for example:

- friend = one syllable = <u>friend</u>
- friendly = two syllables = <u>friend/ly</u>
- friendliest = three syllables = <u>friend/li/est</u>

Singular

Singular is when we write about one of something, for example: <u>*friend*</u>.

Plural

Plural is when we write about more than one of something, for example: <u>*friends*</u>.

A bit confusing, right?

Well, don't worry. You don't need to learn these off by heart. You can use this glossary whenever you come across these words. You'll soon get to know them.

Like most things, the more often you do it the more familiar they become and the easier they are to remember.

Introduction to the activities

All the activities in this book are linked to sessions you may be taught. Obviously this will depend on which level you are working at. To make it easier to find the activities you want the book has been divided into levels. Within each level the activities have been divided into sessions. At the top of each page there is a box like this:

> **This activity relates to:**
> **Entry level three, session 4**

This box tells you which level and session the activity relates to.

Your tutor will refer to this when he or she gives you extra work to do in the sessions or in your own time. It will also help you to monitor your progress.

When you have completed an activity (or two!) ask your tutor to check it for you.

If you are starting, say, at entry level three, there is no reason why you should not do the activities from the previous levels. You know what they say – 'Practice makes perfect.'

Activities for Entry Level One

Activity 1.1

- What do you read?

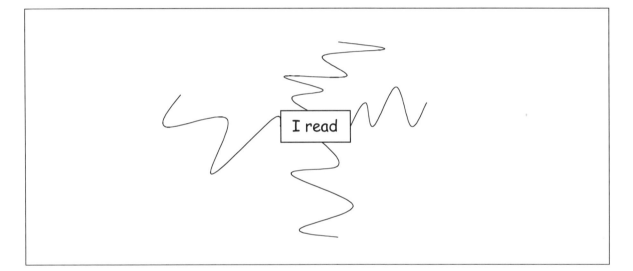

- Why do you read it?

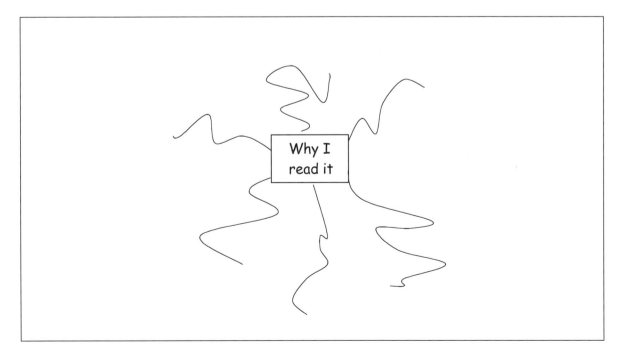

This activity relates to:
Entry level one, session 1

Activity 1.2

Below is a registration form you need to fill in to register at the college library. Have a go at filling it in.

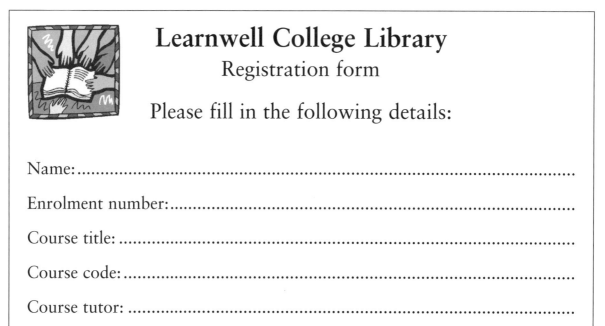

Learnwell College Library
Registration form

Please fill in the following details:

Name: ....

Enrolment number: ....

Course title: ....

Course code: ....

Course tutor: ....

This activity relates to:
Entry level one, session 2

REMEMBER:
the alphabet consists of twenty-six letters in a sequence

Activity 1.3

In the panel below the letters of the alphabet are in a mess. Put them into the correct order in the second panel.

REMEMBER:
Each letter of the alphabet can be written in UPPER CASE and lower case letters

h	m	a	c	j	d	b	f	l	k	g	e	i	x	p	n	v	y	q	o	s	z	w	t	r	u

Activity 1.4

Fill in the missing letters to complete the alphabets.

	B	C		F		H				M	N	O			R	S		V			Z
	a	b	c			g	h		k				q		r				w		

This activity relates to:
Entry level one, session 3

Activity 1.5

In the text in the box below some of the capital letters have been missed out. Can you put them where they should be? What are they used for?

There are twenty-five missing capital letters.

Diary of a childcare student

Today is monday. I was at college today. I met gail at 8.30 am at the bus stop on hampton road. We caught the bus to college and had a coffee before lessons.

Our first lesson today was with Miss blackwood, it was about children's language development. we learnt about a theory by a man called vygotsky. After break we had mr. Lee for foundations to caring. He told us about food hygiene.

After lunch we had miss jacobs for child health. Next week, on tuesday, we are going on a visit to the getwell quick child health clinic. i am really looking forward to that. gail and I have arranged to meet and catch the bus there together.

After college I met my boyfriend, steve, we went to the eatwell café for tea and then I went home.

When I got home my little brother was doing his homework so i helped him with it. When we had finished we watched the football on tv. It was arsenal against tottenham – it was a good match, arsenal won!

These activities relate to:
Entry level one, sessions 4 and 5

Activity 1.6

List the twenty-one consonants here.

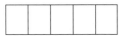

List the five vowels here.

Which letter can be used as a vowel or a consonant?

> **REMEMBER:**
> There are twenty-six letters in the alphabet; twenty-one of them are consonants, five are vowels

This activity is linked to:
Entry level one, session 4

Activity 1.7

Recognising UPPER and lower case letters

The two lists of words in the box below contain words that you will come across in your training.

Each word is written in UPPER CASE and lower case letters. Can you match them up? One has been done for you.

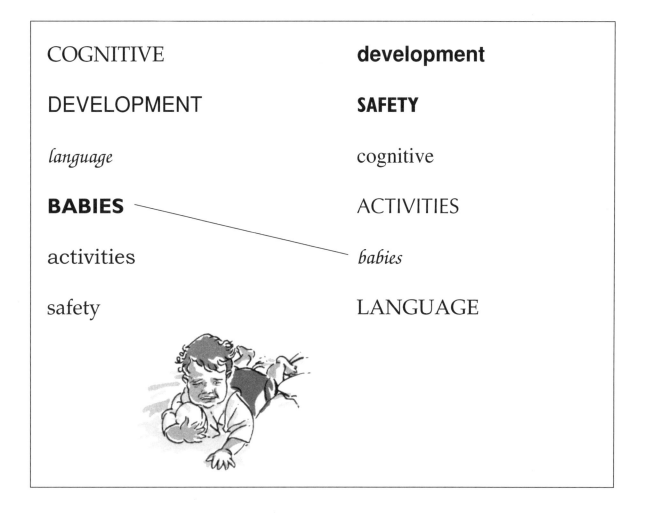

COGNITIVE   **development**

DEVELOPMENT   **SAFETY**

language   cognitive

BABIES   ACTIVITIES

activities   *babies*

safety   LANGUAGE

This activity is linked to:
Entry level one, sessions 4/5

Activity 1.8

Make some consonant–vowel-consonant words in the table opposite.

⇨ You can do this by adding consonants to the vowels and vowels to the consonants.

⇨ There are two spare rows for you to make up some of your own.

Add consonants here				Add vowels here		
	a			m		p
	e			p		t
	i			t		b
	o			s		n
	u			n		t

This activity relates to:
Entry level one, sessions 4/5

Activity 1.9

Which of the words in the box below are using their short vowel sound?

The vowels in each word are highlighted for you.

There are ten words using their short vowel sound. Write them in the table below at the foot of the box.

pl**a**y	m**a**t	h**i**s	**o**nly
on	r**e**st	w**i**ll	t**i**me
an	**u**p	w**e**	m**a**de
th**e**m	c**u**t	n**o**t	n**i**ght

Consonant sounds

The next few pages are linked to session 6.

They are pages for you to add words to whenever you come across them.

They are for ongoing use so you can come back to them whenever you want to.

There is an example of each word using the different consonant sound in each box.

The sound of 'f' as in food

'f' football	'ff' giraffe
'gh' laugh	'ph' pheasant

*The gira*ff*e lau*gh*ed at the* ph*easant playing* f*ootball.*

The sound of 'g' as in girl

'gg' egg	'g' girl
'gu' guitar	'gh' ghost

The g*irl played a* gu*itar while the* gh*ost fried an e*gg*.*

The sound of 'j' as in jump

'dg' bridge	'g' giant	'j' jump

The giant jumped over the bridge.

The sound of 's' as in social

'ce' mice	'sc' scent
's' snake	'ss' hiss

The mice scented the cheese but the snake hissed and scared them away.

The sound of 'k' as in king

'c' cat	'cc' accordion	'ch' echo	'ck' duck
'k' kilt	'qu' queen	'que' cheque	

The sound of the du<u>ck</u> and the <u>c</u>at playing accordions e<u>ch</u>oed around the hall. The <u>qu</u>een said they looked handsome in their <u>k</u>ilts and paid them with a che<u>que</u>.

The sound of 'sh' as in share

'ch' machine	'ci' special	's' sugar	'sh' shampoo
'si' pension	'ssi' mission	'ss' pressure	'ti' nation

The agent was on a spe<u>ci</u>al mi<u>ss</u>ion to save the na<u>ti</u>on.	The ma<u>ch</u>ine put <u>s</u>ugar in the <u>sh</u>ampoo.	The rabbit was under <u>pressure</u> to collect grandma's pen<u>si</u>on.

The sound of 'z' as in zebra

'z'	's'
lazy	daisy

The la<u>z</u>y dai<u>s</u>y snoo<u>z</u>ed in the sun.

This activity is related to:
Entry level one, session 6

Activity 1.10

Here are some words you will come across on your course. Some have the initial consonant clusters missing, some have the final consonant clusters missing.
    Try putting them in.

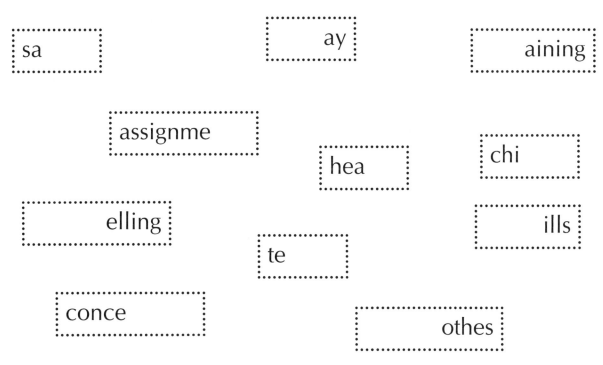

sa

ay

aining

assignme

hea

chi

elling

te

ills

conce

othes

This activity relates to:
Entry level one, session 8

Activity 1.11

This activity is about personal keywords. These are words that you use/see a lot and that are personal to you.

Fill in the details below

First name:..

Second name:..

Where I was born:...

Date of birth (in words): ....

Name of the road I live in: ....

Name of the town or city I live in:..

Children's names: ....

Best friend's name: ....

Where my best friend lives:..

This activity relates to:
Entry level one, session 9

REMINDER!

⇨ Sentences are basic units of writing.
⇨ Every sentence is an idea or group of ideas which is complete on its own.
⇨ Every sentence contains at least one subject – and information about the subject(s) (predicate).
⇨ At the heart of every sentence is a verb – an action word.
⇨ There are different types of sentence, at this stage we are concentrating on 'simple sentences'.
⇨ Simple sentences contain only one subject and one predicate.

For example:

<u>**The baby**</u> *was crying.*
<u>**Subject**</u>   *predicate*

Activity 1.12

Write some simple sentences using the following subjects:

- the children
- the dog
- the lecture

What subject could you add to these predicates?

- it is raining.
- are doing an assignment.
- has some useful books.

Activities for Entry Level Two

This is an alphabet recap activity

Activity 2.1

Here is a list of children who attend Playdays Nursery. Their names need to be put into a register in alphabetical order.

Using only the first letters of the names, put them on the register. Some of the capital letters have been left off. Write those in too.

Christina, Rachael, emma, Margaret, isma, roswana, talvinder, Shabnam, lynsey, Bushra, sobia, Noreen, linda, Samreen, skunthla.

Add your own name to the register as well.

PLAYDAYS NURSERY
REGISTER

NAME	ATTENDANCE MARK							
1								
2								
3								
4								
5								
6								
7								
8								
9								
10								
11								
12								
13								
14								

This activity is related to:
Entry level two, session 1

Activity 2.2

Spelling is . . .

- Something we do every day.

- Something we may need to help the children with at placement.

- Something everyone can do to some level – *Yes you can!*.

- Something we need to get right if we want people to understand what we write.

- Something we need to do to get meaning from reading.

- 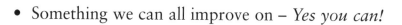 Important but *only one part of writing*.

- Hard to do because English is a complicated language.

- Something we can all improve on – *Yes you can!*

- Setting out letters in the right order to make words. Words need to be spelt correctly to sound right.

Sounds easy, but I can't do it.

YES YOU CAN!

Activity 2.3

Think about it.

What do we need to be able to do to spell correctly?

Have a go at putting a few ideas into the mind map below.

There's an example to start you off.

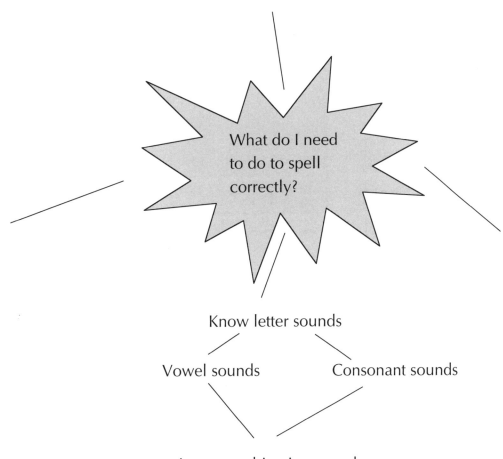

What do I need
to do to spell
correctly?

Know letter sounds

Vowel sounds   Consonant sounds

Letter combination sounds

When you have finished, put a star by the ones you think you need to work on the most.

Literacy for Childcare Students

This activity is related to:
Entry level two, session 2

Activity 2.4

Vowel phoneme search

See how many words you can find in this grid that have the vowel phonemes 'ee', 'ea', 'oa', 'ow', 'y' and 'igh' in them.

The answers may be found at the end of level 2 activities, p. 28.

Put the words into lists according to the vowel phoneme they use.

f	e	e	t	v	b	n	l	w	q	d	r	t	s	d
p	e	s	d	r	t	y	o	v	b	n	m	o	q	a
f	s	k	a	s	t	r	e	e	w	e	r	w	t	y
z	x	y	t	v	b	n	f	f	r	v	b	n	n	n
m	n	b	v	x	z	t	r	e	a	t	g	g	g	h
y	h	n	n	s	r	f	v	t	g	b	e	q	m	z
f	d	d	s	e	v	b	n	m	l	o	p	e	e	w
r	c	s	s	e	s	h	o	w	f	p	o	o	a	k
o	f	d	d	g	t	y	u	i	o	p	l	a	t	s
w	l	x	x	z	c	v	b	m	t	e	a	m	m	t
n	o	s	s	s	d	w	q	a	x	b	n	m	l	k
t	a	y	u	s	i	g	h	u	c	l	o	w	n	s
l	t	h	g	d	s	g	e	a	h	t	t	r	e	a
x	u	r	y	e	e	t	r	c	o	a	t	o	i	m
n	i	g	h	t	z	o	x	k	k	l	b	s	e	a
z	x	v	b	m	k	w	l	h	f	r	o	w	q	q
e	c	r	y	w	q	e	h	g	j	l	a	f	r	s
d	f	g	h	j	l	l	k	p	o	u	t	t	r	e

This activity related to:
Entry level two, session 2

Activity 2.5

How many three- and four-letter words can you make out of the words in the boxes below?

LEARNING

DEVELOPMENT

STORYTIME

ASSIGNMENT

Ideas for practice

Two fun ways of practising making words are:

1. Building a word pyramid. Start with a two-letter word and then build it into a longer word by adding one new letter at a time. For example:

an

and

hand

handy

shandy

2. Changing one letter of a word at a time to make new words:

bat

rat

cat

cap

tap

top

pop

cop

cup

pup

You can make these activities even more fun by having a competition with a friend to see who can get the biggest/most words.

> **This activity relates to:**
> **Entry level two, session 4**

Activity 2.6

Happening or happened?

Look at the sentences below.

Which ones are written in the past tense and which are written in the present tense?

- The children played noisily.
- The school is having a summer fair today.
- Kargill is changing the baby's nappy.
- Samreen went to India in the summer.
- Roswana had prepared lots of activities for the children to do.
- Margaret is reading a story to the children.
- Noreen listened carefully to her tutor.
- Isma told her tutor how much she enjoys working with babies.

**This activity relates to:
Entry level two, session 5**

Activity 2.7

Verbs

Try putting some verbs into their past and present tense.

**REMEMBER
VERBS?**
Verbs are
words that
describe an
action.

Verbs past

How many
verbs can you
think of?

Verbs present

This activity relates to:
Entry level two, session 6

Activity 2.8

REMEMBER NOUNS?
Words that give names to something?

REMEMBER ADJECTIVES?
Words that are used to give more information!

Nouns and adjectives

In the table below there are ten nouns. What adjectives could you add to them to make them more descriptive?

A couple have been done to start you off.

NOUN	ADJECTIVES		
Book	'BORING'		
Paint			
Sandwich			
Biscuit			
Nappy	'SMELLY'		
Easel			
Paintbrush			
Box			
Nursery nurse	'HAPPY'		
Assignment			

This activity relates to:
Entry level two, session 7

Activity 2.9

Tips on forming sentences

Use familiar short words rather than long, unfamiliar ones.

- ☒ To facilitate its use and access.
- ☑ To make it easier to use.

Use accurate words rather than vague ones.

- ☒ This chapter contains several activities.
- ☑ This chapter contains seven activities.

Use brief phrasing rather than long-winded phrasing.

☒ Although as a nursery nurse you should encourage all children to take part in messy activities, you cannot force them. In the end it is up to them to choose what they wish to do.

☑ As a nursery nurse you cannot force children to do messy activities, they do have a choice.

Avoid descriptive, flowery writing unless it adds information which the reader needs to know.

☒ As we are all aware, young children of this age can be very ego-centric (self-centred).

☑ Young children can be very ego-centric (self-centred) at this age.

In other words, be direct, be interesting!

> **This activity relates to:**
> **Entry level two, session 7**

Activity 2.10

Sentence Building

Simple sentences are very useful but when used a lot they can make your writing sound disjointed and 'bitty'.

Have a look at what is written in the box below; the text is composed of simple sentences. Where could you join some of the sentences together with a conjunction (joining word)?

Does it sound better?

Today is Monday. It is snowing. Not many children came today. At playtime we went outside. It has stopped snowing. The children enjoyed playing in the snow.

After playtime we went back inside. We had a warm drink. We had a biscuit. The children sat on their cushions. I read them a story about a snowman.

We painted pictures of the snow. Some children painted snowmen. Others painted the snow falling.

The children were excited at home time. They couldn't wait to get out into the snow again.

This activity relates to:
Entry level two, session 8

Activity 2.11

Filling in the gaps

Have a go at writing a short piece of text for each of these pictures. Maybe you can write a little story for some young children, a few lines to persuade someone that they want to go to this place.

Think about the different texts you have looked at in lessons and the language they use. Use a mixture of simple and compound sentences.

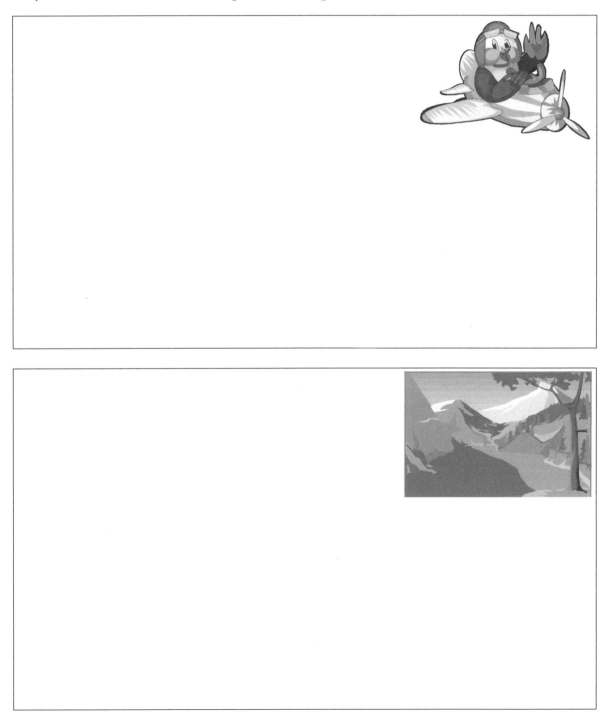

**This activity relates to:
Entry level two, session 9**

Activity 2.12

Where to find it!

Below are two lists. The first is a list of information, the second a list of texts where you can find information.

Link the information to where you could find it.

Buses to town	Poster
Child development theories	Leaflet
Assignment details	Tutorial sheet
Targets for the term	Timetable
Local playgroup times	Financial newspaper
Showing times for a film	Textbook
Football match report	Course handbook
Stocks and shares information	Local newspaper
Wedding announcement	Sports pages of a newspaper

Activity 2.13

I'll tell you how to get there

You have invited everyone to your place for a party.

A couple of your friends live near the college but do not know how to get to your place. Write out some instructions for them.

Here's how to get to my place!

Answers to vowel search on p.18.

f	e	e	t	v	b	n	l	w	q	d	r	t	s	d
p	e	s	d	r	t	y	o	v	b	n	m	o	q	a
f	s	k	a	s	t	r	e	e	w	e	r	w	t	y
z	x	y	t	v	b	n	f	f	r	v	b	n	n	n
m	n	b	v	x	z	t	r	e	a	t	g	g	g	h
y	h	n	n	s	r	f	v	t	g	b	e	q	m	z
f	d	d	s	e	v	b	n	m	l	o	p	e	e	w
r	c	s	s	e	s	h	o	w	f	p	o	o	a	k
o	f	d	d	g	t	y	u	i	o	p	l	a	t	s
w	l	x	x	z	c	v	b	m	t	e	a	m	m	t
n	o	s	s	s	d	w	q	a	x	b	n	m	l	k
t	a	y	u	s	i	g	h	u	c	l	o	w	n	s
l	t	h	g	d	s	g	e	a	h	t	t	r	e	a
x	u	r	y	e	e	t	r	c	o	a	t	o	i	m
n	i	g	h	t	z	o	x	k	k	l	b	s	e	a
z	x	v	b	m	k	w	l	h	f	r	o	w	q	q
e	c	r	y	w	q	e	h	g	j	l	a	f	r	s
d	f	g	h	j	l	l	k	p	o	u	t	t	r	e

Activities for Entry Level Three

This activity relates to:
Entry level three, session 1

Activity 3.1

Sentences

What is the *subject* of each of the following sentences?

1 Childcare students will be at placement next week.
2 Jean Piaget wrote a theory about how children learn.
3 Children are usually walking by the time they reach their first birthday.
4 The assignments about children's language development were quite hard to do.

What is the *verb* in each of the following sentences?

5 We will be learning about childhood illness on this course.
6 We are going to visit a health centre next week.
7 I handed in my assignment on Monday of last week.
8 Children need to play outside so that they can run around, let off steam, develop their gross-motor skills and get some fresh air into their lungs.

What tense are each of the eight sentences above written in? List them below.

	PAST	PRESENT	FUTURE
1			
2			
3			
4			
5			
6			
7			
8			

This activity relates to:
Entry level three, session 1

Activity 3.2

What am I?

Add a prefix or suffix to the word in the box to make a word that matches the meaning given.

⇨ This word is used to show children's work:

> *play*

⇨ This word is used to describe what the nursery nurse is doing when she tells children a story from a book:

> *read*

⇨ This is the word for something children produce with pencils and paper:

> *draw*

⇨ This is the word for where students go to get their practical experience:

> *place*

This activity relates to:
Entry level three, session 2

Activity 3.3

Building sentences

We have looked at making words, sentences and text in lessons.

Think of writing text in the same way as building a wall.

The words are bricks, sentences are rows of bricks and we add rows until the wall or text is complete.

Here's an example:

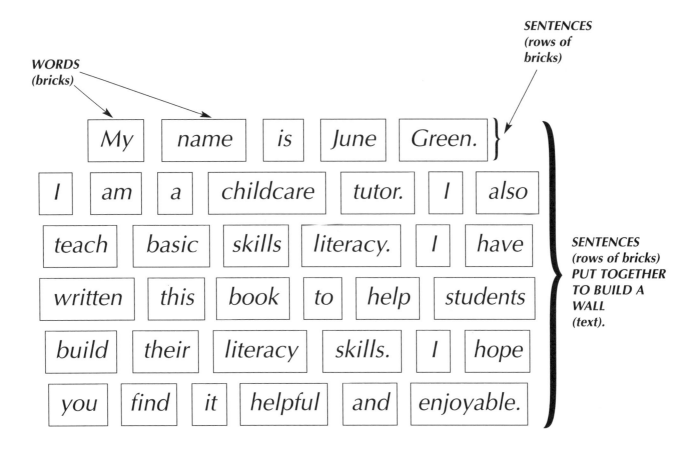

WORDS
(bricks)

SENTENCES
(rows of bricks)

My | name | is | June | Green. }

I | am | a | childcare | tutor. | I | also

teach | basic | skills | literacy. | I | have

written | this | book | to | help | students

build | their | literacy | skills. | I | hope

you | find | it | helpful | and | enjoyable.

SENTENCES
(rows of bricks)
**PUT TOGETHER
TO BUILD A
WALL**
(text).

Have a go at building your own:

Wall of text

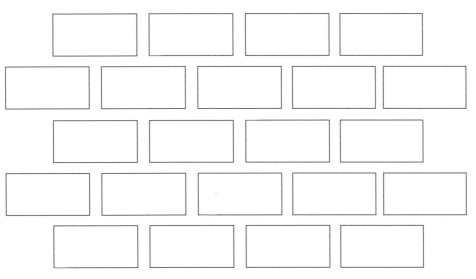

Activity 3.4

Using speech marks and commas

The box below contains a letter to parents about a residential trip that some children are going on. You have been asked to read it through and check punctuation.

Letter to parents

Dear parents

Regarding the residential trip to Oxford As you know the children will be camping out for two of the nights they are there I would be grateful if you would make sure that your child has the following equipment for camping a warm sleeping bag warm nightclothes a few changes of socks waterproof jacket and trousers two changes of clothing and underwear toiletries and a torch

   We look forward to taking this trip with the children and would like to assure you of their safety and well-being while they are away with us

   Should you have any queries please do not hesitate to contact me

Yours sincerely

Stephanie Lee
Deputy head-teacher

This activity relates to:
Entry level three, session 3

Activity 3.5

Writing speech

Carry out a short observation of two people or children having a conversation. While you are observing them make notes on what they are saying to each other.

When you have done this write up your observation, indicating clearly what they have said, with the use of speech marks.

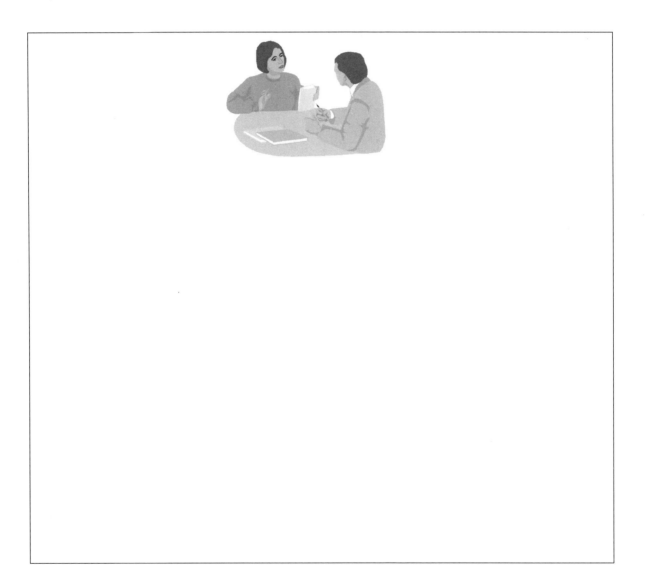

Activity 3.6

Skimming and scanning

Go through a newspaper and skim for four headlines that catch your attention.
   Either photocopy or cut out the articles that caught your attention.
   Why did these articles catch your attention?

⇨
⇨
⇨
⇨

Now scan them for interest. Which two would you like to read in detail and why?
   What do you think they are about?

⇨
⇨

Now read each article in detail.
   What was it about?

Was there anything in the article that you did not expect to be there? What was it?

Why would you not expect it to be there?

Write a short summary of each article.

This activity relates to:
Entry level three, session 5

Activity 3.7

Looking for information

For this activity you will need a copy of the *A–Z* for your area and a local telephone directory.

In the telephone directory look up the following:

- Nearest hospital, with an accident & emergency department, to home or college.
- Nearest playgroup and day nursery.
- Nearest primary school.
- Find these places in the *A–Z* and work out the route from home/college to them.

1 Explain in writing how you found them.

2 Write out the directions for someone new to the area.

This activity relates to:
Entry level three, session 6

Activity 3.8

Writing styles

In session 6 you looked at different styles of writing and did some activities about it.

For this activity complete the following pieces of writing. Think about what you learned in session 6 when doing this.

1 You have seen this advertisement in the local paper:

• Write a letter asking for more detail and an application form.

NURSERY NURSES

We are looking for committed, forward-thinking
staff for our new nursery.
The nursery will cater for children aged 0–4 years.

INTERESTED??
Please contact Gail
at
Happyones
Head Office
High Street
Birmingham

2 In response to your letter Happyones have asked you to write to them giving details about yourself.

• Write a letter in reply giving the details you think they should have.

This activity relates to:
Entry level three, session 6

Activity 3.9

Now have fun with these!

Design a party invitation! This could be your party or a children's party.

Party invitation

Design a playgroup newsletter. It should include something about a fundraising event or a recent visit from the fire brigade.

Playgroup newsletter

Note

There are no extension activities for session 7 as the session has a large task attached to it; this will take some time to do.

Activities for Level One

This activity relates to:
Level one, session 1

Activity 1

Dictionary and thesaurus practice

In the box on the next page there is some information about childhood immunisation. There are quite a few unfamiliar words in it.

⇨ Use a dictionary to find out their meaning.
⇨ Then use a glossary from a child health book to find out their meaning.
⇨ Write them down in the table below.
⇨ Are they very different?

Word	Dictionary meaning	Glossary meaning

Childhood immunisation

Immunisation is when vaccines are used to protect people from diseases.

Vaccines contain either very small, weakened parts of the virus or bacteria that cause the disease or small parts of the toxins the virus/bacteria produce. These minute parts have been treated to prevent the disease from occurring, but they make the body produce the relevant antibodies to protect against the disease.

Because babies and young children are particularly vulnerable to these diseases they are given a programme of immunisations very early in life. The immunisations will protect children from the diseases and prevent the disease from being passed to others if it does occur. Children who are not immunised are more at risk of contracting the disease.

Below is the immunisation schedule for children up to the age of 5.

AGE	IMMUNISATION	METHOD
2 months	# HIB (Meningitis) # Diptheria, whooping cough, tetanus # Polio	One injection One injection By mouth
3 months	Same as 2 months	Same as 2 months
4 months	Same as 2 and 3 months	Same as 2 and 3 months
12 to 15 months	# Measles, mumps, rubella (MMR)	One injection
3 to 5 years	# Diptheria, whooping cough, tetanus # Polio # MMR	Given by same method as before. These are the ***Pre-school boosters***, given to boost immunity before children start school

This activity relates to:
Level one, session 2

Activity 2

Word families

In session 2 of level one you looked at word families.

Have a look at the handout, 'Childhood immunisation', used in the previous activity.

Can you spot the two words that are in the family belonging to the word *immunise*?

The following activities are about words connected to child health.

In each of the tables below there is a word.

Find the other words belonging to the word family, then look up their meanings in a dictionary. Can you see how they are related?

REMINDER!
Word families are groups of words that contain the same root word.

Health	MEANING

Ill	MEANING

Immunise	MEANING

Infect	MEANING

This activity relates to:
Level one, session 3

Activity 3

Apostrophes

What are the apostrophes used for in the sentences below?

- The film's music was very good.
- They're very quiet today.
- Wasn't the end-of-term party good fun?
- Today is the students' placement day.

What's been missed out in the following sentences?

- The nursery nurse was comforting the child, who wasnt very well.
- Roswana is happy because shes nearly completed her course.
- 'Were all looking forward to the exam being over', said the students.
- Flippers is a great fish n chip restaurant.

Now try writing some sentences or phrases that show the different uses of apostrophes.

This activity relates to:
Level one, session 3

Activity 4

Commas

What are the commas used for in the sentences below?

- Kargill wanted to read a story, but the children wanted to sing some rhymes.
- Most children will crawl before they walk. However, some will miss out the crawling stage altogether.
- Topics that could be used to stimulate discussion with children are what children did at the weekend, talking about parties, a recent trip or their favourite TV programme.
- Thank you, everyone, for an interesting discussion.
- The little boy said, 'I was scared of the fire engine 'cos it was so loud'.

Now try writing a sentence or phrase that shows the use of commas.

This activity relates to:
Level one, session 4

Activity 5

The text in the box below is about a child (singular) and his reaction to going on a school trip. Rewrite the text as if you were writing about the whole (plural) class.

The school trip

The little boy is excited because he is going on a school trip today. I asked him what he was most looking forward to. 'Seeing the robots', he replied. 'I'm going to make a light bulb work with electricity', he said.

When we got to the museum he went off with his group, chattering away and exclaiming loudly, 'Look Miss, look at that!'

The class met up at lunchtime and he was very excited. 'Miss', he exclaimed, 'I talked to a robot, I told it a joke and it laughed.'

**This activity relates to:
Level one, session 4**

Activity 6

Working with homophones

Below are some common homophones. They are also the ones people get most confused with!

Use each of them in a sentence.

REMINDER!
Homophones are words that sound the same but mean something different.

there	where	off	to	here
their	wear	of	too	hear
	were		two	

Note

There are no extension activities for session 5 as the session has a large task attached to it; this will take some time to do.

This activity relates to:
Level one, session 6

Activity 6

Who am I?

A personal profile is something you write that tells someone all about you as a person.

It could include: age, likes, dislikes, personality, hopes, achievements, family, friends and so on.

Your task is to write your own personal profile.

1 Put into spidergram format what you want to include in your profile.
2 Write out your profile.
   Remember to check:

   ➪ punctuation
   ➪ spelling
   ➪ grammar
   ➪ paragraph structure
   ➪ sense and meaning.

This activity relates to:
Level one, session 6

Activity 6

Punctuate these

Remember the work you have done on punctuation? Have a go at punctuating the sentences in the boxes below. Check back to the punctuation section in this book if you get stuck.

would you like me to come in with you

to work effectively you will need to understand the roles of those you work with

examples of objects that might be used are
wooden spoons
cones
pieces of textured fabric
shells
natural sponges

im too lazy to be a celebrity he says

this book is gails

babies and young children can be given any type of object that will be safe for them to touch hold and in the case of babies put into their mouths

the stages and sequences of physical development

tell you what he said feigning innocence

Note

The activities on the next few pages are not linked to a particular session. They have been set for you to work on your reading comprehension.

Activity 9

Reading comprehension

⇨ Comprehension is about understanding.

⇨ If you do not understand what you read, the text loses its meaning for you.

⇨ Comprehension is very important when doing a course. On most courses there is lots of reading to do and understand. On your childcare course, for example, you need to read developmental theories, child development, assignments, handouts, lecture notes and so on.

Let's think about assignments.

- You need to understand exactly what you have to do – if you don't you could get it wrong and fail!
- Assignments are very wordy and often contain a lot of technical, jargonistic words. Even more reason why it is important to understand them.
- Skimming and scanning are good techniques that will help you to understand.

The activity on the opposite page is based on an assignment task. You will see the assignment task and then some questions to answer that will check your comprehension of the task.

1 Skim the assignment.
2 Read the questions.
3 Scan the text, looking for keywords that are linked to the assignment. These keywords will help you to answer the questions.

Assignment task

This task is about childhood illness.

You are expected to show your knowledge of the two childhood illnesses stated by completing the task. The two illnesses on which your task is based are:

⇨ Chicken-pox
⇨ Asthma

Your work should include the following:

PART ONE

⇨ Identify the causes of both illnesses.
⇨ Describe the signs and symptoms of each illness.
⇨ Explain how to care for a child with these illnesses.

PART TWO

⇨ Explain how these illnesses can be prevented or controlled.

PART THREE

⇨ Describe any national or local strategies to prevent illness in children.

PART FOUR

⇨ Describe the effect of long-term illness on a child and the child's family.

You must complete all four parts of the task.
Your word limit is 3000 words.

Activity 10

Comprehension check

Answer the following questions about the assignment.

1 What area of childcare is the assignment about?

2 What is the assignment specifically about?

3 What does your work need to include?

4 List the keywords that give you specific instructions.

5 How many words can you use?

6 What do you have to do to complete the task?

Activity 10

What is it saying?

One of the most influential things we read is advertisements.

People who are clever with words and graphics write advertisements. They use words, pictures and so on. to persuade people to buy, try or give something.

Holiday brochures are one example. Beautiful pictures and descriptive writing are used to persuade you that this is where you should spend those precious holiday weeks.

Have a look at the ad on the opposite page.

1 What thoughts and feelings does it provoke?
2 What sort of holiday is it for?
3 What sort of place is it?
4 Which words and phrases are used to persuade you to go there?

Holiday Ad

Are you looking for a holiday of peace and quiet? Beautiful scenery, places that take you back to a time long ago?

Then this is the place for you!

Breathtaking scenery by day and by night

Romantic sunsets

Historical landmarks taking you back in time.

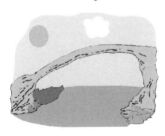

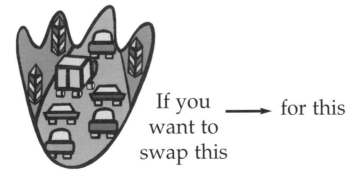

If you want to swap this ⟶ for this

this is the place for you!

Activities for Level Two

This activity relates to:
Level two, session 1

Activity 1

Complex sentences

In session one of level one you did some work on complex sentences, so called because they are very complex.

Find some information about Bruner's theory of learning and a more recent theory, for example, Sandra Scarr (1992).

1 Read both theories and identify the simple, compound and complex sentences in them.
2 Pick one of each sentence type and compare the structure, and the amount of information in them. Identify the clauses, subjects and verbs within each sentence.
3 Read the two theories in detail and make a note of any differences and similarities. Write a short summary of the two theories, making sure you use some complex sentences.

Try putting your notes in the format on the following page and see how it works for you.

REMINDER!
There are three types of sentence:
• *Simple*, one subject, one clause.
• *Compound*, two clauses joined by a conjunction.
• *Complex*, based on a main clause, with more than one subordinate clause to support the main clause.

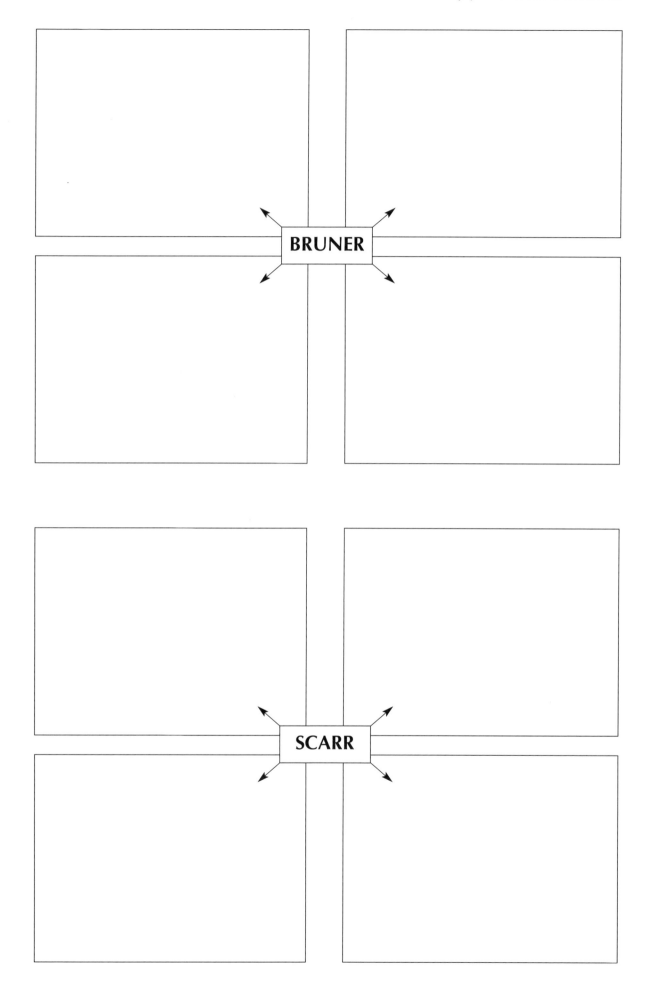

This activity relates to:
Level two, session 1

Using complex sentences

Write a complex sentence about each of the following:

⇨ Your course

```



```

⇨ Child development

```



```

⇨ Your favourite film or book or both

```



```

This activity relates to:
Level two, session 2

Activity 2

Poetry

In session 2 you looked at different text types. We kept poetry for now!
    Poetry is an excellent source of different types of text.

⇨ Poems are written by people to express thoughts, feelings, ideas, opinions and so on through words they have chosen very carefully.
⇨ Poems can be happy, sad, emotional, humorous and even nonsense.
⇨ Some poets use rhythm and rhyme in their writing. This is when there is about the same number of syllables in each line. This gives it the rhythm and the word at the end of the line will rhyme.
⇨ Other poets use rhyme alone, when words at the end of the lines rhyme.

If you have never felt like exploring poetry start with some children's verse – it is excellent and sometimes very, very funny!

Exercise

• Find four poems that you could work with.
• Try to include at least one humorous and one serious, and two about the same subject. This could be the weather, an animal, children or a special occasion.
• Read them and then fill in the chart on the next page.

Title of poem	What type of poem is it?	What is it about?	Does it use rhythm and rhyme or just rhyme?	What is your opinion? Give your reasons.

This activity relates to:
Level two, session 2

Activity 3

Using descriptive writing

The words we use when we write can make our writing interesting – or not!

This activity is to encourage you to use more descriptive words when you write. There are two activities for you to complete. Be at your most descriptive!

Imagine yourself in your very favourite place

WHAT CAN I SEE?   WHAT CAN I HEAR?

MY FAVOURITE PLACE

WHAT CAN I SMELL?   HOW DO I FEEL?

Using the idea of your favourite place, write four paragraphs that describe this place in detail.

⇨ Use the four headings as your paragraph guides.
⇨ Use as much descriptive language as you can.
⇨ Write it as if you were trying to persuade someone to go there.
⇨ Let loose the creative side of you!

**This activity relates to:
Level two, session 3**

Activity 4

What type of text?

In session 3 you looked at the different purposes of text.

The following two activities are to encourage your skills at deciding what type of text you are reading.

Exercise

Read the following pieces of text and decide what their purpose is.

Is the purpose to retell, persuade, inform, discuss, give points of view?

TEXT ONE

The second-year students will not be at college next week as they have an extra week at placement.

TEXT TWO

In the session on caring for babies last week, we were shown how to bath a baby and put on their nappy.

Most of us were all fingers and thumbs when we had a go. It's a good job we weren't bathing real babies!

As for putting on terry-towelling nappies – forget it. Every time I lifted my 'baby' up – the nappy fell off. It's disposables for me!

TEXT THREE

Nature or nurture?
The debate goes on. How do we learn to behave and build our social skills?

One group of theorists believes that we behave and learn in ways according to our genetic make-up. That what we inherit from our parents makes us who we are.

Another group would have us believe that it is our environment that is most influential. That we will learn and behave the way we see others around us doing.

Yet another group would have us think that while our genes do play a part in how we turn out, the environment also has an influence.

What do you think – nature, nurture or a bit of both?

Note

There are no specific activities linked to sessions 4, 5 and 6 of Level two. There is already an extensive task that uses lots of the skills you have developed. On the next few pages you will find some activities that will give you some revision opportunities – never a bad thing.

So sit back and enjoy this little 'break'.

Revision opportunities

Below is a filled-in crossword. The answers are all to do with child development. Write a clue for each answer.

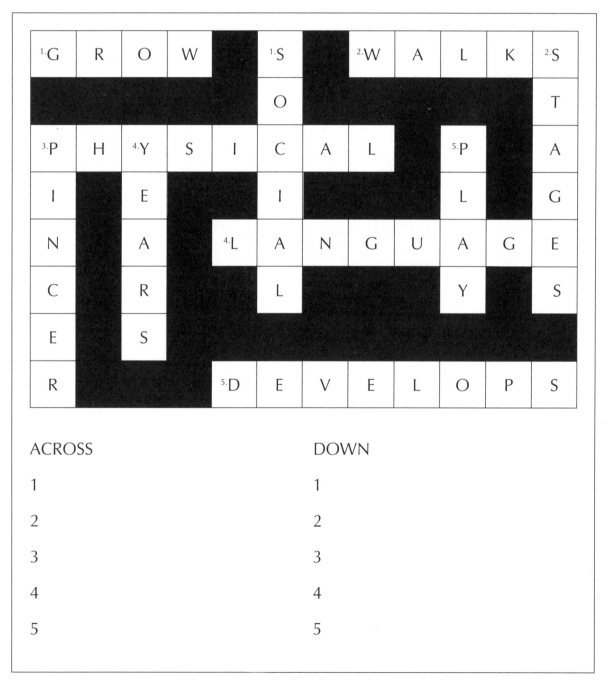

ACROSS

1

2

3

4

5

DOWN

1

2

3

4

5

Root words

What are the root words for the following word families?

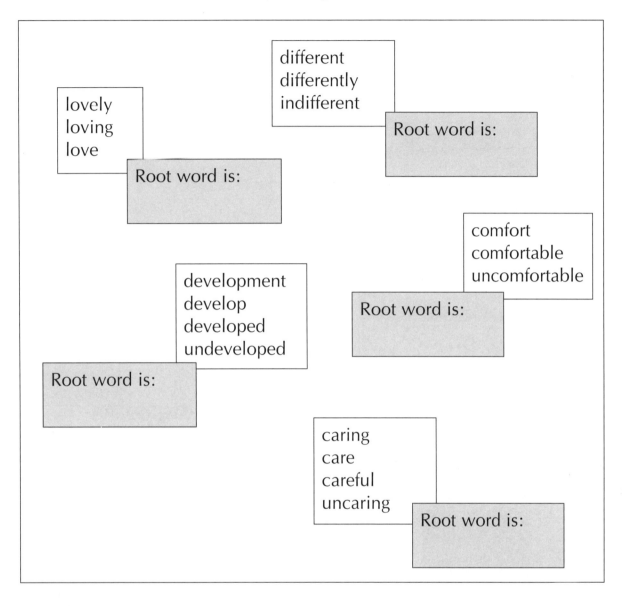

Synonyms

Find some synonyms for these words:

- look

- complex

- style

- example

- theory

Verbs

All the words in the table below are verbs. Fill in the missing vowel to complete the verb.

W		L	K		N	G	■	■	R
	■	■		■	■	■	■	■	
	■	■	C	■	■	■	R		N
T		L	K		N	G	■	■	■
	■	■		■	■	■		S	K
N	■	■	N	■	■	■	■		■
G	■	■	G	R		W		N	G
■	■	■	■	■	■	■	■	G	■

Abbreviations

An abbreviation is a shortened version of something. For example, you will have seen *etc.* used on your handouts and in other places. It is short for '*et cetera*'. It means there is more you could add, so when you see etc. used it means that some examples have been given but there are more that could be added/used.

If you notice, you will see there is always a full stop after the abbreviation *etc.* This happens with many other abbreviations.

Have a look at the abbreviations listed below. What do they stand for?

- RSVP

- NSPCC

- MP

- QCA

- e.g.

- i.e.

> **This activity relates to:**
> **Level two, session 8**

Activity 5

In session 8 you looked at how arguments are presented. You explored the language used and how they are set out.

Exercise

Think of an issue you have a strong feeling about. It could be an environmental issue, a difference of opinion, you may disagree strongly with something you have read about child development theory or it could be a local issue.

Write a letter to a newspaper stating your argument.

It may help you to make some notes first. For example:

⇨ What is my issue?
⇨ Why do I feel this way?
⇨ What evidence can I give to support my argument?
⇨ Who would this issue affect – if anyone – or is it just something I do not agree with?
⇨ What are the effects of the action I am against?
⇨ What are the most important points that I need to get across in this letter?
⇨ What type of language should I use?

Obviously not all of these will be relevant to you, it depends on your issue. These are just to give you some ideas.

When you have completed your letter why not send it off? Wouldn't it be great to see your letter published? Go on, give it a go – *I dare you!*

**This activity relates to:
Level two, session 9**

Activity 6

Writing speech

When we are writing about what someone is saying we tend to use the word '*said*' a lot.

* Skunthla *said* the room was cold.

This could be written as:

* Skunthla *complained* the room was cold.

Use a thesaurus to find as many words as you can to use instead of *said*.

⇨ Try using some of them by writing out some fictitious speech.
⇨ How do they make a difference to your writing?
⇨ Which ones sound dramatic, which ones sound soft?

Remember this in your future writing.

Spelling rules

The next few pages are all about spelling rules.

- Spelling rules help us to make our writing make sense.
- Spelling rules help us to spell.

There are a few spelling rules and your tutor will go over them with you. My advice would be to keep revisiting them until you know them without having to look them up. As with spelling, a little bit every day is better than a big chunk once a week.

You will have covered some of them in lessons, especially rules for adding prefixes and suffixes – but it's good to have them all in one place for easy reference, plus a bit of revision is good for you.

Honest it is!

Changing singular words into plurals

Most words are made into plurals by simply adding an 's':

- toy – toys   book – books   paint – paints

However, take a look at these:

- Glass – glasss   box – boxs   push – pushs

    Do they look right? Can you pronounce them?

They don't look right and they are difficult to pronounce, aren't they?
    That's because there are rules for adding 's' to words.

Changing words ending 's', 'ss', 'x', 'sh', 'z', 'zz', 'ch' and 'tch' into plurals

When a word ends in 's', 'ss', 'x', 'z', 'zz', 'sh' or 'tch' you need to add 'es'; for example:

- glass – glasses   box – boxes   push – pushes
- buzz – buzzes   touch – touches   watch – watches

When changing a word that ends with the soft sound of 'ch' add 'es'; for example:

- chur<u>ch</u> – chur<u>ches</u>

When changing a word that ends in the hard sound of 'ch' simply add an 's'; for example:

- monar<u>ch</u> – monar<u>chs</u>:

Changing words ending 'y' into plurals

When you want to make a word that ends in 'y' a plural you need to look at the letter before the 'y' to know whether to add 'es' or 's'. Here's the rule:

- If the letter before the 'y' is a vowel simply add an 's'; for example, 'to<u>y</u>' becomes 'to<u>ys</u>' and pla<u>y</u> becomes 'pla<u>ys</u>'.

If the letter before the 'y' is a consonant, change the 'y' to 'i' and add 'es'; for example, stor<u>y</u> becomes 'stor<u>ies</u>' and 'bab<u>y</u>' becomes 'bab<u>ies</u>'.

Changing words ending 'f', 'fe' and 'ff' into plurals

When you want to make a word that ends in 'f' or 'fe' a plural:

⇨ Most of them drop the 'f' or 'fe' and change to 'ves'; for example, hal<u>f</u> – hal<u>ves</u>; scar<u>f</u> – scar<u>ves</u>; li<u>fe</u> – li<u>ves</u>; shel<u>f</u> – shel<u>ves</u>.

⇨ A few of them just need an 's' added; for example, roo<u>f</u> – roo<u>fs</u>; chie<u>f</u> – chie<u>fs</u>; sa<u>fe</u> – sa<u>fes</u>.

You can tell which way to change the word by saying it out loud to yourself. You will be able to tell by the sound of the word whether you should simply add an 's' or change it to 'ves'.

⇨ When making a word that ends in 'ff' a plural, simply add an 's'; for example, cli<u>ff</u> – cli<u>ffs</u>; sni<u>ff</u> – sni<u>ffs</u>.

Changing words ending in 'o' into plurals

Normally you just need to add an 's'; for example, pian<u>o</u> – pian<u>os</u>.
There are a few words that need an 'es' added; for example:

potato – potatoes	volcano – volcanoes
tomato – tomatoes	torpedo – torpedoes
go – goes	echo – echoes
halo – haloes	domino – dominoes
hero – heroes	buffalo – buffaloes

cargo – cargoes   grotto – grottoes
mango – mangoes   motto – mottoes
tornado – tornadoes   mosquito – mosquitoes

There is no rule for these – it's just the way they are!
  Try and remember them or refer back to this page when using them.

Words that change completely to become plurals

child – children   foot – feet
woman – women   tooth – teeth
man – men   goose – geese
mouse – mice

Again no rule – just how it is!

That's it for changing singulars to plurals
('At last!' I hear you cry).

Now we'll take a look at some rules for adding prefixes and suffixes to root words.

REMINDER!
Prefixes are added to the beginning of words to make a new word. Suffixes are added to the end of words to make a new word.

Adding '-ed' and '-ing' to words

When we use verbs we change them to suit the sentence we are using them in. For example:

REMINDER!
Verbs are action words

- The children like to *paint*.
- The children *painted* yesterday.
- The children will be *painting* tomorrow.

Usually you only need to add '**-ing**' or '**-ed**' to the verb to change it.
  There are some exceptions and here are the rules for them.

⇨ If the verb has one syllable, a long vowel sound, ends in 'e', remove the 'e' and add 'ed' or 'ing'; for example:

bak*e* – bak*ed* – bak*ing*

⇨ If the verb has one syllable, a short vowel sound, ends in a consonant, you should double the consonant and add '*ed*' or '*ing*'; for example:

na*p* – na*pped* – na*pping*

Words that have more than one syllable and end in a single consonant.

⇨ If the stress is on the last syllable, double the consonant and add '*ed*' or '*ing*'; for example:

> admi*t* – admi*tted* – admi*tting*

⇨ If the stress is not on the last syllable just add '*ed*' or '*ing*'; for example:

Words that end in 'l'.

⇨ For words that have only a single vowel before the 'l' simply add '*led*' or '*ling*'; for example:

> pe*dal* – peda*lled* – peda*lling*

⇨ For words that contain a double vowel before the 'l', just add '*ed*' or '*ing*'; for example:

> spoi*l* – spoi*led* – spoi*ling*

Words that end in 'y'.

⇨ If a word has a vowel before the 'y', simply add '*ed*' or '*ing*'; for example:

> play – play*ing* – play*ed*

⇨ If the word has a consonant before the 'i', change the 'y' to an 'i' before adding '*ed*' but leave it as a 'y' if adding '*ing*'; for example:

> dry – dr*ying* – dr*ied*

Adding 'ly' to words

When we add 'ly' to a word we are changing an adjective into an adverb.

⇨ Most of the time, when we want to add '*ly*' to a word, we can just add it; for example:

> He is a *quiet* reader
> He reads *quietly*

However, there are some differences – here are the rules!

⇨ If you want to add '*ly*' to a word that ends in 'll', just add 'y'; for example:

> hi*ll* – hi*lly*

➡ If you want to add '*ly*' to a word that has more than one syllable and ends in a 'y' drop the 'y' and add '*ily*'; for example:

> funn*y* – funn*ily*

➡ If you want to add 'ly' to one-syllable words that end in 'y', you usually just add the '*ly*'; for example:

> sly – sly*ly*

Again there are some exceptions; here they are:

> gay – ga*ily*
> day – da*ily*

➡ If you want to add '*ly*' to a word ending in 'le', drop the 'e' and add 'y'; for example:

> pimple – pimp*ly*

Adding '-ful' to words

➡ When you add '*full*' to a word, it loses the second 'l'; for example:

> hope – hope*ful*
> play – play*ful*

That's it for adding suffixes.

Now for prefixes

The good news is there aren't many rules for adding prefixes!
Here they are:

➡ When you want to use the prefixes '*mis*', '*un*' and '*dis*' DON'T change a thing about the root word; for example:

> approve – disapprove
> happy – unhappy
> treat – mistreat

➡ When you want to use '*all*' as a prefix drop the second 'l' before you use it; for example:

> together – altogether
> ways – always

That's it for prefixes!

There are just two little rules left to look at.

The 'ie'/'ei' rule

This rule is quite easy to remember:

⇨ '<u>i</u>' before '<u>e</u>' except after '<u>c</u>' – when the sound is '<u>ee</u>'; for example:

ach*ie*ve	rel*ie*f
re*ce*ive	per*ce*ive

Is it – ce or se?

This is another easy rule to try and remember. It is:

⇨ '<u>c</u>' for a noun and '<u>s</u>' for a verb; for example:

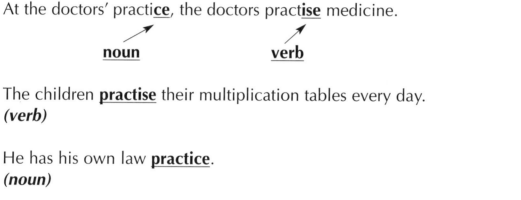

At the doctors' practi**ce**, the doctors practi**se** medicine.

                noun   **verb**

The children **practise** their multiplication tables every day.
(verb)

He has his own law **practice**.
(noun)

I'm sure you'll be pleased to know – that's it for spelling rules. It sounds long-winded I know, but try learning a few at a time.
   You'll be surprised how they help your spelling skills.

Spelling quiz

Every week or so you will be doing a spelling quiz.
The following page is for you to photocopy as many times as
you wish and to do the quizzes on.
Use a separate half-page for each week's quiz.

You will be able to see how much you are progressing week
by week and also keep track of those awkward words that
are difficult to get your head around. We all have them!

GOOD LUCK!

DATE

DATE

Dictionary

Get some blank sheets of paper or a notebook and make your own dictionary. Put the letter of the alphabet at the top (see example on next page).

You can use them to record words you find difficult to spell and unusual words you come across.

Have fun with it!

Thesaurus

In the later levels of the course you will have learned how to use a thesaurus.

Get some blank sheets of paper and record your own thesaurus.

You can then use it as an easy reference point when you get stuck for a word.

Parts of speech

Remember those 'parts of speech' you learned about in lessons?

This section of the book is for you to record words that come into each of those groups.

There is a page for each: nouns, adverbs, adjectives, pronouns, adverbs, conjunctions.

Use these pages to record words when you come across them. It will help you to remember what they are and when to use them.

NOUNS

VERBS

ADVERBS

ADJECTIVES

PRONOUNS

CONJUNCTIONS (joining words)

Reading diary

The next few pages are for you to use as a reading diary.

You should try and read a variety of books, both fiction and non-fiction as well as magazines and newspapers. Anything you read broadens your experience of the written word and will influence you in your own writing.

Besides which it is great fun!

Every book you read will be different; some you will enjoy, some you won't.

It may be the topic, the way it was written or something you just can't put your finger on.

Keeping a diary can be a good way of finding out which sorts of books suit you best.

You will find some pointers on the next page to get you going. After that it's up to you!

BOOK TITLE

AUTHOR

TYPE OF BOOK (FICTION/NON-FICTION)

WHAT WAS IT ABOUT?
For fiction books – what was the storyline, main characters(s), setting, etc.

WHAT DID YOU LIKE ABOUT IT?

WHAT DID YOU NOT LIKE?

WOULD YOU READ A BOOK BY THIS AUTHOR AGAIN?

WHY?